BASKETBALL LEGENDS

Kareem Abdul Jabbar

Larry Bird

Wilt Chamberlain

Julius Erving

Magic Johnson

Michael Jordan

CHELSEA HOUSE PUBLISHERS

BASKETBALL LEGENDS

WILT CHAMBERLAIN

Ron Frankl

Introduction by
Chuck Daly

CHELSEA HOUSE PUBLISHERS
New York · Philadelphia

Produced by Daniel Bial Agency
New York, New York.

Picture research by Alan Gottlieb
Cover illustration by Peter Fiore

First Printing

1 3 5 7 9 8 6 4 2

Frankl, Ron.
    Wilt Chamberlain / Ron Frankl.
       p.   cm. — (Basketball legends)
    Includes bibliographical references and index.
    ISBN 0-7910-2428-8 (hard)
    1. Chamberlain, Wilt, 1936–   —Juvenile literature.
2. Basketball players—United States—Biography—Juvenile
literature. [1. Chamberlain, Wilt, 1936–   . 2. Basketball
players. 3. Afro-Americans—Biography.] I. Title. II. Series.
GV884.C5F73 1994
796.323′092—dc20
[B]   94-5775
                                                    CIP
                                                    AC

CONTENTS

BECOMING A BASKETBALL LEGEND 6
Chuck Daly

CHAPTER 1
AN UNSTOPPABLE FORCE 9

CHAPTER 2
BASKETBALL PRODIGY 17

CHAPTER 3
KANSAS DAYS 25

CHAPTER 4
NOBODY ROOTS FOR GOLIATH 33

CHAPTER 5
I SACRIFICED MY SCORING 41

CHAPTER 6
A RETURNING HERO 49

CHAPTER 7
AFTER THE GAME 57

STATISTICS 61
CHRONOLOGY 62
FURTHER READING 63
INDEX 64

BECOMING A
BASKETBALL LEGEND

Chuck Daly

What does it take to be a basketball superstar? Two of the three things it takes are easy to spot. Any great athlete must have excellent skills and tremendous dedication. The third quality needed is much harder to define, or even put in words. Others call it leadership or desire to win, but I'm not sure that explains it fully. This third quality relates to the athlete's thinking process, a certain mentality and work ethic. One can coach athletic skills, and while few superstars need outside influence to help keep them dedicated, it is possible for a coach to offer some well-timed words in order to keep that athlete fully motivated. But a coach can do no more than appeal to a player's will to win; how much that player is then capable of ensuring victory is up to his own internal workings.

In recent times, we have been fortunate to have seen some of the best to play the game. Larry Bird, Magic Johnson, and Michael Jordan had all three components of superstardom in full measure. They brought their teams to numerous championships, and made the players around them better. (They also made their coaches look smart.)

I myself coached a player who belongs in that class, Isiah Thomas, who helped lead the Detroit Pistons to consecutive NBA crowns. Isiah is not tall—he's just over six feet—but he could do whatever he wanted with the ball. And what he wanted to do most was lead and win.

All the players I mentioned above and those whom this

series will chronicle are tremendously gifted athletes, but for the most part, you can't play professional basketball at all unless you have excellent skills. And few players get to stay on their team unless they are willing to dedicate themselves to improving their talents even more, learning about their opponents, and finding a way to join with their teammates and win.

It's that third element that separates the good player from the superstar, the memorable players from the legends of the game. Superstars know when to take over the game. If the situation calls for a defensive stop, the superstars stand up and do it. If the situation calls for a key pass, they make it. And if the situation calls for a big shot, they want the ball. They don't want the ball simply because of their own glory or ego. Instead they know—and their teammates know—that they are the ones who can deliver, regardless of the pressure.

The words "legend" and "superstar" are often tossed around without real meaning. Taking a hard look at some of those who truly can be classified as "legends" can provide insight into the things that brought them to that level. All of them developed their legacy over numerous seasons of play, even if certain games will always stand out in the memories of those who saw them. Those games typically featured amazing feats of all-around play. No matter how great the fans thought the superstars, the players were capable yet of surprising them, their opponents, and occasionally even themselves. The desire to win took over, and with their dedication and athletic skills already in place, they were capable of the most astonishing achievements.

CHUCK DALY, currently the head coach of the New Jersey Nets, guided the Detroit Pistons to two straight NBA championships, in 1989 and 1990. He earned a gold medal as coach of the 1992 U.S. Olympic basketball team—the so-called "Dream Team"—and was inducted into the Pro Basketball Hall of Fame in 1994.

1
AN UNSTOPPABLE FORCE

It was the most remarkable performance in the history of the National Basketball Association. Wilt Chamberlain, the 25-year old center of the Philadelphia Warriors, was awesome as he put shot after shot through the basket. Ever since he had turned pro, Chamberlain dominated opposing centers on a nightly basis and established himself as the greatest scorer and rebounder the game had ever seen. On this night, basketball's greatest young talent surpassed his own usual high standards.

It was March 2, 1962, and the Warriors were playing the New York Knicks in Hershey, Pennsylvania, a small city (about an hour from Philadelphia) where the Warriors played several games every season. An enthusiastic crowd of over 4,000 fans had turned out for the opportunity to see Wilt Chamberlain, the NBA's star attraction.

Chamberlain was leading the league in

When Wilt Chamberlain wanted to score, no one could stop him.

scoring and rebounding for the third consecutive season. He was averaging 50 points per game, an astounding total in a sport where scoring 20 points is considered a good performance and 30 points is considered a great one. In the 1961-62 season, Wilt Chamberlain would go on to score more than 50 points in 45 games, a remarkable feat.

By mid-season, he had broken the single-game scoring record twice, hitting for 73 points early in the season, then pouring in 78 in a game in December. With every tipoff, he threatened to break the scoring record again.

His offensive abilities were so overpowering that the league had already made several rule changes aimed at reducing Chamberlain's domination, although they had had little effect. Wilt Chamberlain was an unstoppable force, and neither opposing players nor changes in the rule book could alter this situation.

At 7' 1¾" and about 250 pounds, the muscular Chamberlain was the strongest player in the NBA. But it was more than his height and strength that set him apart. Unlike many big men in basketball at the time, Chamberlain was a tremendous athlete, with the reflexes and foot speed usually found only in much smaller players. He could run, jump, and shoot as well as any man in the league. His rebounding skills were unsurpassed, and he was the most fearsome shot blocker in the game.

Chamberlain seldom missed games due to injury, and he usually played all 48 minutes of every game. Most amazingly, during the 1961-62 season he sat out only 8 minutes 33 seconds of one game, after getting ejected for arguing an official's call. He played every other minute of every game. Because some of the Warriors' games had gone into overtime, Chamberlain actually averaged *more* than 48 minutes of play per game over the course of the 82-game season.

On this night, the Knicks quickly discovered that they were powerless to stop Chamberlain, as he used his enormous size and strength to score almost at will. By the end of the first quarter he had scored 23 points, a fine total for an entire game for most basketball players.

Chamberlain added another 18 points in the second quarter, giving him a total of 41 at halftime. He also pulled down 14 rebounds, as his Warriors led the Knicks by the score 79-68. Chamberlain succeeded on 14 of his 26 shot attempts, a respectable if unremarkable field goal percentage. More surprisingly, he had hit 13 of his 14 free throws, overcoming his usual struggles from the foul line. With such an excellent first half, Chamberlain had an excellent chance to equal or break his scoring record of 78 points.

The Knicks were one of the NBA's weaker teams, and their center, Darrell Imhoff, was no match for Chamberlain. The 6'11" Imhoff got into foul trouble early in the first half and was

Wilt rewards himself with some milk after setting the NBA's all-time single-game scoring record with his 100-point performance on March 2, 1962.

forced to leave the game. The shorter players who took turns replacing him in the Knicks' lineup were incapable of defending against the mighty Chamberlain.

There had been other big men who had excelled at the center position before Chamberlain. George Mikan of the Minneapolis Lakers, a great scorer and rebounder, dominated the NBA's early years. More recently, the Boston Celtics' Bill Russell, a defensive specialist, had established himself as one of the league's best players and led his team to the league championship in four of the previous five seasons.

The on-court battles between Chamberlain and Russell had already become legendary, with the Philadelphia center usually dominating the scoring and rebounding, but with Russell and his Celtics usually winning the game. The Celtics were the best-coached and hardest-working team in the league, with a wealth of talented and unselfish players.

Despite Boston's successes, it seemed to be only a matter of time before Chamberlain would lead the Warriors to the first of a series of championships. Chamberlain's abilities on the court were so great that some observers believed that Chamberlain could lead

The battles between rival centers Chamberlain and Bill Russell (right) were as great as any seen in basketball.

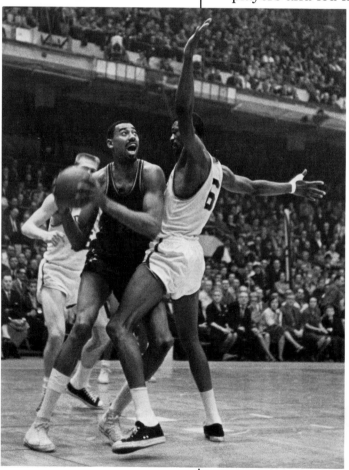

even a mediocre team to the NBA title.

Due to poor coaching and inconsistent play, the Warriors had been eliminated from the playoffs in the early rounds in Chamberlain's first two seasons. Chamberlain had often feuded with his coach, Neil Johnston. But Johnston had been fired after the previous season. With new coach Frank McGuire, the Warriors finally had a leader who recognized Chamberlain's intelligence and sensitivity, and who also realized that keeping his talented young center happy was essential to winning.

There was one problem with Chamberlain's style of play. His domination was so complete that after his teammates passed the ball to Chamberlain they were often reduced to the role of on-court spectators. Tonight, as usual, guards Guy Rodgers and Al Attles brought the ball upcourt and passed it to Chamberlain under the basket on almost every possession. The big center rarely passed the ball back outside to his teammates, none of whom were very reliable shooters. Instead, even with two, three, or four defenders pressuring him, Chamberlain would take the shot. Using his size, strength, and quickness, Chamberlain would still find a way to make the basket.

When the Warriors and the Knicks returned to the floor to begin the second half, Chamberlain resumed his awesome scoring demonstration. The Knicks' overmatched defenders were tiring badly. To stop Chamberlain from scoring, they were forced to foul him almost every time he got the basketball. This sent the Philadelphia center to the foul line again and again. Normally a poor free-throw shooter, Chamberlain made 15 of his 18 free throws in the second half. Meanwhile, he continued his hot shooting from the field, and he entered the fourth quarter with 69 points, and the Warriors leading by a comfortable margin of 125-106.

With the outcome of the game no longer in doubt, Chamberlain's teammates continued to feed the ball to their star center. The crowd was in a frenzy, as they realized that they were witnessing a historic performance. With eight minutes left in the game, he broke his own single-game scoring record of 78. Chamberlain and the Warriors then set their sights on the seemingly impossible goal of 100 points.

With almost all of their players in serious foul trouble, the Knicks were reduced to holding the ball for as long as possible and using up as much of the time on the 24-second clock to keep the basketball out of Chamberlain's hands. None of the Knicks' efforts mattered, as Chamberlain continued his assault, quickly reaching 80 points, then 90. The fans screamed with excitement with each basket.

With less than a minute left to play, Chamberlain missed a short jump shot. Teammate Joe Rucklick grabbed the rebound and passed the ball back inside to Chamberlain. With 46 seconds remaining, he hit an easy lay-up for his 99th and 100th points. The cheering crowd surged onto the floor, and the game was halted as the fans and players on both teams congratulated Chamberlain on his amazing achievement. They had witnessed the greatest offensive performance in NBA history. So great was the uproar that play was not resumed, and the last 46 seconds were never played.

No other player, before or after, has come close to equalling Chamberlain's 100-point mark. David Thompson scored 73 points in a game in 1978, and Pistol Pete Maravich reached 68 in a game in 1977. Chamberlain himself hit for 70 in 1963 and 68 in 1967. This is as near as any player has come to challenging Wilt Chamberlain's single-game scoring record.

In the locker room after the game, Chamberlain was, surprisingly, less than pleased with his historic performance. He was embarrassed to have taken 63 shots, (of which he made 36), because it made him sound like a selfish player. "You take that many shots on the playground and no one ever wants you on their team," Chamberlain said. He did not consider it to be the best game he had ever played, preferring instead a game on November 24, 1960, in which he pulled down an incredible 55 rebounds.

Years later, however, Wilt Chamberlain grew to appreciate the significance of his 100-point performance. "I like the 100-point game more than I did at the time," he said. "It has reached fabled proportion, almost like a Paul Bunyan story, and it's nice to be a part of a fable."

2
BASKETBALL PRODIGY

Wilton Norman Chamberlain was born in Philadelphia, Pennsylvania, on August 21, 1936, one of 11 children. Wilt was the only one in the family who grew to an unusual height. His parents, William and Olivia, were both less than 5' 10", and the tallest of Wilt's two brothers grew to 6' 5". By the time he was eight years old, it was already obvious that Wilt would be very tall. When he graduated from the sixth grade, he was already 6' 3".

Wilt's parents worked hard to support their large family. William worked first as a welder in a shipyard, then as a janitor and handyman. He also held part-time jobs and earned extra money doing small jobs in their neighborhood. Wilt's mother, Olivia, worked full time cleaning other family's homes, while also doing the cooking, cleaning, and other duties in her own household.

All of the Chamberlain children were as-

As a high school track star, Wilt ran the half mile in two minutes and set local records in the shotput.

signed chores to perform in their home. At an early age they were encouraged to find part-time jobs. They turned over their earnings to their parents' without complaint to help with expenses. Wilt did chores and odd jobs for neighbors. Later, he started his own junk business, recycling valuable metal and other materials from other people's trash. He also sold fruit, painted fences and houses, and did construction work while he was still a youth.

Wilt at age 12, "just before I grew my beard."

The Chamberlains were certainly not wealthy, but due to their hard work, they always had all the necessities. "My folks managed. They didn't deny us anything that mattered," Chamberlain recalled years later. "We always had clothes on our backs and food on the table."

Wilt and his family lived in a mostly black, working-class neighborhood of West Philadelphia. The family was close, and Wilt remembered his childhood as a very happy one. "My parents always had time for us. They taught us right from wrong. None of us went wrong, and we were raised in a neighborhood where a lot of kids went wrong."

As a child, Wilt had some serious health problems. He developed a hernia that required surgery when he was still a toddler. He also developed pneumonia and almost died when he was in the fourth grade, and he missed so many days of school that he had to repeat the grade. Later, as a teenager, he developed a serious and painful problem with infected mosquito bites on his legs.

As a teenager, Wilt continued to grow, but he did not enjoy the attention he drew because of his height. Nearly seven feet tall at the age of 14, Chamberlain was uncomfortable with the stares and comments that he attracted. He was bright but sensitive, and wished he could be treated like everyone else. Chamberlain did not enjoy being treated as a curiosity or a freak. Even as an adult, he resented the cruelty of strangers, who often annoyed him with nasty and thoughtless remarks such as "How's the weather up there?"

Wilt was always athletic and well coordinated, despite his height. Even in his youth he was very competitive, and he sought to excel at every sport he tried. Running was his favorite sport. Wilt and his neighborhood friends ran everywhere they went, with Chamberlain's unusually long legs giving him a great advantage. He became a high school track-and-field star, one of the best in Philadelphia. He competed in the 440 and 880 yard runs, the high jump, and the shotput.

Surprisingly, Wilt showed little interest in basketball as a boy and only began playing the sport when he reached junior high school. Typically, when he decided to try the game, he worked hard at it every day, developing his skills through many hours of practice.

Before he even began high school, Chamberlain led his YMCA basketball team to victory, first in the Philadelphia tournament, then to the national YMCA championship. This was a major accomplishment. Most of the players in the national tournament were college players, and Chamberlain outplayed opponents who were much older. Although he had yet to play his first high school game, Wilt Chamberlain had begun to attract the attention of high school and college coaches, NBA scouts, and other basketball experts.

Despite offers to play at other Philadelphia high schools, Chamberlain chose to attend his neighborhood school, Overbrook High School. He chose Overbrook so he could play with his four best friends. By their senior year, Chamberlain and his friends had become the starting five of the Overbrook basketball team.

Chamberlain and his Overbrook teammates had great success over the course of his three years on the school's varsity team. The team had a record of 58 wins and only 3 losses. They won Philadelphia's public school championship in Chamberlain's first season and captured both the public and city championships in his junior and senior years.

The greatest high school basketball talent that Philadelphia had ever seen, Chamberlain rewrote all of the city's scoring records. No opposing team could stop him. He regularly scored 40 or 50 points per game, even though high school games lasted only 32 minutes. (College games are 40 minutes, and professional games run 48 minutes). Often, Overbrook had such a large lead that the coach asked Chamberlain to sit on the bench and give less talented teammates a chance to play in the second half.

Chamberlain's greatest talent was his inside scoring ability, as he could hit his shots almost

The high school senior makes the sport look like child's play during a game in 1956.

every time he got the ball underneath the basket. And although he was still slender and had not developed the enormous strength he would possess as a pro, Chamberlain was already an awesome rebounder and shot blocker. He also would sometimes bring the ball upcourt after a rebound, demonstrating surprising agility as a dribbler and a passer. At this point in his playing career, Chamberlain was also a good outside shooter. He would surprise defenders with his soft jump shot from 20 feet or more from the basket, an unusual skill for a center.

Coaches and recruiters from nearly 200 colleges and universities came to every game and tried to talk with Wilt and his family constantly. He was the first high school basketball player to be so widely recruited, a "can't miss" talent who could turn any school into a national contender. Eventually, Overbrook's basketball coach, Cecil Mosenson, assumed the responsibility of supervising the recruiters' contact with Chamberlain and his family.

By his senior year, colleges were flying him in to visit their school, paying all his expenses, putting him up in top hotels, and treating him to fine meals. Some schools secretly offered the young man cash, cars, and other gifts for choosing their institution. This was a serious violation of NCAA (National Collegiate Athletic Association, the governing body of college sports) rules, and several of the schools were later questioned by the NCAA and the FBI.

After much consideration, Chamberlain chose Kansas University, located in the small midwestern city of Lawrence, Kansas. Some experts were surprised at his choice, because Kansas was not a basketball powerhouse. Chamberlain made his choice because he wished to play for Phog Allen, one of the greatest coaches in basketball history. Allen had coached since 1920 and had learned the game from Dr. James Naismith, who had invented the game of basketball and had later become the athletic director at Kansas. Allen was a smart and likable man who quickly earned Chamberlain's trust on the basis of their several meetings.

Professional scouts and coaches had also followed Chamberlain's development, convinced that the high school star would soon become a standout in the NBA. Eddie Gottlieb, the owner of the Philadelphia Warriors, was so convinced of Chamberlain's ability that he selected Chamberlain, a high school senior, in the NBA college draft. NBA rules prohibited the young center from playing in the league for another four years, when his class was scheduled to graduate from college, but Gottlieb was willing to wait.

Gottlieb befriended Chamberlain and arranged a summer job for the young man at Kutsher's Country Club, a resort hotel in the Catskill Mountains in New York State. Chamberlain had an enjoyable summer, working part time as a bellhop. He spent the remainder of his time playing in Kutsher's summer basketball league, where he played for Red Auerbach, coach of the Boston Celtics. Kutsher's attracted some of the leading college and NBA stars, and Chamberlain outplayed everyone he faced on the court, much to the embarrassment of some of the older players.

With high school behind him, Wilt Chamberlain was clearly headed for greatness. The basketball world eagerly awaited his debut at Kansas.

3

KANSAS DAYS

Wilt Chamberlain was eager to begin his enrollment at Kansas University, and the school was equally excited over the arrival of their prize recruit. A serious problem developed, however, even before he arrived on the university's campus.

On his first night in Lawrence, where the university was located, Chamberlain and a black friend went to a restaurant. Although the owner recognized Chamberlain as the university's new basketball star, his restaurant was for whites only. He would not let them in the main room, although he offered to serve them in the kitchen. Chamberlain was so shocked to encounter such racial discrimination that he considered going home.

Although segregation was still practiced in many parts of the country, Chamberlain had not faced it while growing up in Philadelphia. Chamberlain decided he would not accept seg-

Chamberlain's all around talents made him an instant success at Kansas University.

25

regation in Lawrence. Either the policy would change, or he would leave.

Coach Allen persuaded Chamberlain to remain in Lawrence. Allen and some influential alumni of Kansas University encouraged local businesses to change their policy and admit black customers. Vowing to use his fame to bring integration to Kansas, Chamberlain claims to have visited nearly every restaurant in the Lawrence area, and there were no further incidents. Other blacks followed his example, and many of the racial barriers around the town soon came down.

Chamberlain settled quickly into college life. He enjoyed his college courses and took classes that were more challenging than many athletes choose to take. He was an adequate student who discovered that he enjoyed learning, although his grades grew worse as he devoted much time to basketball. Chamberlain also hosted a radio show on the campus radio station.

Freshmen were not allowed to compete on varsity teams at the time, so Chamberlain was forced to spend a year playing on the freshman team. The freshman squad, led by its 7' 1"center, easily defeated every team it played, including the Kansas varsity team. There was tremendous excitement as basketball fans at Kansas and across the country awaited Wilt Chamberlain's first game as a varsity player.

In 1956, basketball coach Phog Allen, who was the primary reason why Chamberlain chose to attend Kansas, reached the age of 70. Despite Allen's long record of success, the university insisted that he follow school policy and retire from coaching. Both Chamberlain and Allen were greatly disappointed that they would

not get to work together on the basketball court, as the two had become very close. The new Kansas coach was Dick Harp, who had been Allen's assistant coach.

Chamberlain made his debut with the Kansas varsity as a sophomore and, as expected, he was tremendous. In his first game, he scored 52 points and pulled down 31 rebounds. Opposing teams were powerless to stop Chamberlain, who dominated the court both on offense and defense. He led the Kansas Jayhawks to a 21-2 record, which included a streak of 12 consecutive wins to open the season. The team won the Big Eight Conference championship and rose to second

As a freshman at Kansas University, Chamberlain shows that his defense could be as dominating as his offense.

in the national rankings behind North Carolina at the end of the season.

Kansas won its first three games of the 1957 NCAA tournament, including a 34 point victory over the 1956 champion, the University of San Francisco. The North Carolina Tarheels survived a scare in their previous game, when they were almost upset in triple overtime by Michigan State. Although North Carolina had few outstanding players, it was a well-trained team led by one of the game's best coaches, Frank McGuire.

The final game between Kansas and North Carolina was a dream match-up between the two top-ranked teams in the country. And the game turned out to be one of the most memorable in the history of the NCAA tournament. Many fans and experts thought that, because of Chamberlain, Kansas was unbeatable. McGuire knew that the key to beating Kansas was to find a way to stop Chamberlain, or at least slow him down a little. If Chamberlain could be contained by the Tar Heels, Kansas had no other players who were capable of assuming the scoring and rebounding burden. McGuire told his team, "We're playing Wilt, not Kansas; just stop him and don't worry about those other guys; they're not all that good."

McGuire designed a defensive strategy to make it more difficult for Chamberlain to receive the ball from his teammates and to get off his shots. The North Carolina center guarded Chamberlain closely at all times, and every time Chamberlain would go up for a shot, the Tar Heel center and two forwards moved between Chamberlain and the basket. The presence of three defenders under the basket made it more difficult for Chamberlain to tip in missed shots and grab rebounds. The constant pressure on Chamberlain, McGuire believed, would tire him out. Also, North Carolina players chose their shots very selectively and took only those they were likely to make, which meant Chamberlain had less opportunity to grab rebounds.

The North Carolina strategy worked at first, and the Tar Heels took an early lead. Although Chamberlain took a fair number of shots, he had to settle for more difficult ones than usual, working hard for every opportunity. At the end of the first half, North Carolina led by the score of 29-22.

Kansas came roaring back and took a three point lead early in the second half. The teams traded the lead several times as the game reached its final minutes. The turning point, it seemed, occurred when the Tar Heels' leading scorer, Lenny Rosenbluth, fouled out of the game with 1:43 left on the game clock and Kansas leading 46-43. It looked as if the Jayhawks had the victory all sewn up.

A poor inbound pass from Kansas' Ron Loneski, however, turned the ball over to North Carolina, which scored a basket and a free throw. Tied at 46 all, the contest headed for overtime.

Both teams grew cautious and chose their shots carefully. Each side scored only one basket, sending the game into a second OT.

As the next overtime began, the tension continued to grow, as the two teams scrapped and clawed for every shot, every rebound, every loose ball. Struggling for a rebound, Chamberlain and Tar Heel Pete Brennan got carried away and began to trade shoves and punches. The two players were quickly separated, and the game was delayed several minutes while the referees restored order.

Finally, in the third overtime, Tar Heel center Joe Quigg hit two free throws to give North Carolina a 54-53 lead with six seconds on the clock. The Jayhawks tried a desperation pass downcourt to Chamberlain, but the ball was knocked away. North Carolina had won the championship. An exhausted Wilt Chamberlain and the Kansas team left the court in shock.

Chamberlain had scored a game-high 23 points and was named the tournament's most valuable player, but this did little to reduce the sting of the loss. Chamberlain later called this game the biggest disappointment of his basketball career.

Chamberlain returned for his junior year at Kansas, but the team had only limited success. The big center felt that, because of his size, referees were allowing opposing players to batter him physically without calling fouls on the offending players. He grew frustrated by the pounding he was receiving in almost every game. He also grew tired of Coach Harp's conservative approach to basketball.

Increasingly unhappy on the basketball court, and with his interest in academics decreasing, Chamberlain decided to leave Kansas at the end of his junior year to pursue an NBA career. The only problem was that NBA rules prohibited Chamberlain from joining the league until his class was scheduled to graduate. It would be another year before Chamberlain could enter the NBA.

Eddie Gottlieb, the owner of the Philadelphia Warriors, the team that held Chamberlain's NBA playing rights, had an idea. Gottlieb introduced Chamberlain to Abe Saperstein. Saperstein owned a small part of the Warriors, but his major claim to fame was that he owned and coached the legendary Harlem Globetrotters.

The Globetrotters were basketball's best-known team. Founded by Saperstein in 1929, the all-black Globetrotters were known as "the clown princes of basketball." Combining basketball skills with comedy, the Globetrotters had toured the world for many years popularizing basketball while entertaining audiences who had never seen the game before. While in later years the Globetrotters stressed their comic antics rather than their basketball skills, in the 1950s they still attracted some of the most talented black players in the game and could beat NBA teams on occasion. Their games often drew larger crowds than NBA games.

Chamberlain had grown up a fan of the Globetrotters. When Saperstein suggested that he join the team, Chamberlain leapt at the opportunity.

Chamberlain spent a year with the Globetrotters. He particularly enjoyed his travels with the team in Europe. He also managed to sharpen his basketball skills. The Globetrotters often used the seven footer as a guard, which gave him the chance to work on his ballhandling and outside shooting, rare talents for a man as huge as Chamberlain. But the Globetrotters' demanding travel schedule, which sometimes included two or even three games a day, took its toll on Chamberlain. He was eager to join the Philadelphia Warriors for the 1959-60 season and begin his NBA career.

Chamberlain poses in 1958 with Abe Saperstein, whose Harlem Globetrotters helped popularize basketball around the world.

4

NOBODY ROOTS FOR GOLIATH

No NBA rookie ever had as large an impact on the league as Wilt Chamberlain. In the 1959-60 season, he led the NBA in scoring with a 37.6 points per game average, then an all-time single-season record. He also hauled down a league-leading 27 rebounds a game. Chamberlain was chosen the NBA's most valuable player, rookie of the year, and he was also named to the All-NBA team. No player had ever won all three honors in the same season.

Sensing Chamberlain's enormous appeal before he had played his first NBA game, the Warriors paid him $65,000 in his first season, the league's highest salary. And the Warriors drew the league's largest crowds, both at home and on the road, as all basketball fans wanted to see what the young center could do.

Despite his inexperience in the NBA, Chamberlain was clearly the best center the league had ever known. He could handle any

Wilt usually outscored and outrebounded Bill Russell in their meetings, but Russell's Celtics usually won.

other center he faced. He was an amazing scorer and rebounder, and he was also capable of playing intimidating defense.

The only major weakness in Chamberlain's game was his free-throw shooting. In practice, he was able to make the shot better than most teammates. In games, however, Chamberlain made only 58 percent of his free throws as a rookie. Opposing teams learned that a good way to stop Chamberlain from scoring was to foul him and make him shoot free throws.

Outside of Chamberlain, most of the Warriors were past their prime. Their coach, Neil Johnston, had no previous experience as a head coach. The Warriors were no match for the league's dominant team, the Boston Celtics.

Red Auerbach, the Celtics' coach, was an innovative leader. The Celtic attack featured guard Bob Cousy, the game's best playmaker.

Chamberlain and Celtic Bill Russell were the NBA's best centers. Russell did not score very much, but the Celtics did not need his scoring for their team to win. He made his contribution with defense, rebounding, and passing.

Many fans and sportswriters saw Russell as the underdog in his match-ups against Chamberlain. Chamberlain himself remarked, "The world is made up of Davids. I am a Goliath. And nobody roots for Goliath." He did not often show his feelings in public, but Chamberlain hated being seen as the villain.

When Chamberlain and Russell faced each other, they brought an extra intensity to the game, and their on-court rivalry inspired both centers to some of their best performances. Chamberlain usually outscored and outrebounded his Boston counterpart, but the

Celtics consistently found a way to win the game. As a result, many regarded Chamberlain's accomplishments as meaningless because he did not lead his team to victory.

When the Warriors and Celtics met in the playoffs at the end of Chamberlain's rookie year, Boston won, four games to two. Despite his inexperience and a badly injured hand, Chamberlain outplayed Russell. But because his team had lost, some began to refer to Chamberlain as a "loser."

This was not fair to Chamberlain. The Warriors' management asked him to score as many points and grab as many rebounds as possible, and he did this with remarkable consistency. But not even Wilt Chamberlain could carry an inferior team to an NBA championship.

Chamberlain also felt that the referees were again allowing opposing players to batter him with vicious and illegal fouls that would have been called if any other player was receiving such mistreatment. Chamberlain was so angered by this physical abuse that he briefly threatened to retire after his first season.

The NBA introduced some new rules specifically to decrease Chamberlain's impact on the game. Offensive goaltending (where a member of the shooting team would touch or deflect the basketball when it was directly over the rim, which was a Chamberlain specialty) was outlawed, and the "three-second rule" (which prohibited an offensive player from staying in the lane in front of his basket for more than three seconds) was added.

In 1961, at the end of Chamberlain's sec-

Chamberlain in his Philadelphia home at the end of his first season after announcing he had played in his last NBA game.

ond NBA season, the Warriors were eliminated in the first round of the playoffs by the Syracuse Nationals. Chamberlain once again captured the scoring and rebounding titles, but he was increasingly unhappy with his coach, Neil Johnston. The two men disagreed on team strategy. Also, Chamberlain preferred to play the entire game, while Johnston sat him on the bench to rest occasionally.

By the beginning of Chamberlain's third season, Johnston was gone. The Warriors' new coach was Frank McGuire, who had coached the North Carolina team that had defeated Chamberlain and the Kansas Jayhawks in the memorable 1957 NCAA championship game. Chamberlain described McGuire as "the finest man and the best coach I've ever played for." He favored an upbeat style of play featuring a lot of running and fast breaks, which was also Chamberlain's preference. McGuire had been a tremendous admirer of Chamberlain since his college days.

McGuire told Chamberlain that he could play the entire game if he wished, and also told him that if he could boost his scoring average to 50 points per game, the Warriors could beat the Celtics. McGuire also complained to the referees when Chamberlain was battered by oppos-

Chamberlain's major flaw: he was not a good free-throw shooter. As a result, he tried many different shooting styles, including releasing the ball underhand.

ing players, which Neil Johnston had never done.

The 1962-63 season was one of Chamberlain's finest. Besides his record 100-point game, his most remarkable achievement was his 50.4 scoring average, which was *12* points better than the all-time record he had set only a year earlier. A group of hardworking players such as guards Guy Rodgers and Al Attles and Tom Meschery now surrounded Chamberlain. With an excellent coach and new talent, the Warriors' future appeared bright.

Philadelphia finished second behind Boston in the regular season and met their archrivals again in the Eastern Conference Finals. In a thrilling series, the Celtics defeated the Warriors by two points in the closing seconds of the seventh and final game. Wilt Chamberlain had lost another opportunity to shake his unfair reputation as a "loser."

Chamberlain was also earning a reputation as a difficult player to coach. He certainly gave each of his coaches more than a few moments of frustration. Chamberlain could be very stubborn, and he sometimes sulked if he could not do things his way. He occasionally made comments in public that upset his teammates, opposing players, or coaches. He also could be incredibly generous and considerate of his teammates.

When it came to the fans, he was unusually patient and polite. He would often remain at courtside after games to sign autographs for all the fans who waited for him, long after all the other players had entered the locker room.

For an athlete, Chamberlain had an unusually wide variety of interests outside of basketball, but travel was one of his favorite activities. For 12 consecutive summers, he rejoined the Harlem Globetrotters for a few weeks of their European tour, which he enjoyed greatly.

In many ways, Chamberlain seemed happiest away from basketball. An intelligent and inquisitive man, he realized that the wealth basketball provided him gave him the chance to do many of the things he enjoyed most in life. He dated many beautiful women and clearly enjoyed his active social life.

The 1962-63 basketball season brought major change to Chamberlain's life. Eddie Gottlieb, the Warrior's owner and a good friend to Chamberlain since the center's high school days, sold the team. The new owners decided to move the team to San Francisco, California, and Chamberlain began his fourth season in the NBA playing in a new city. For family reasons, Frank McGuire chose to remain in the East. Bob Feerick, another former college coach, took over as head coach.

The Warriors struggled in their first year in San Francisco. Chamberlain led the league in scoring and rebounding again, but for the first time in his life, he played for a team with a losing record. The Warriors did not even make the playoffs. Before the next season, Feerick was replaced as coach by Alex Hannum.

Hannum, a former professional player, had been a successful coach in both St. Louis and Syracuse. He believed that strong defense was the key to winning in the NBA. He asked Chamberlain to improve his defensive skills, which had always been less important to him than his offense. He demonstrated strong abilities as a defender and, while he won the scoring title for the fifth consecutive year, he averaged eight points fewer per game than the year before.

Many observers expected Chamberlain and Hannum to have difficulty getting along with each other. Both were strong-willed and emotional, and on one occasion they almost got into a fistfight. The two men, however, worked well together. They respected each other and became good friends off the court.

Hannum's style of basketball led the Warriors to a very successful season. Playing now in the Western Division, the Warriors met the Celtics in the NBA Finals. Chamberlain played brilliantly and completely outplayed Bill Russell, but his efforts were not enough. Boston won its sixth championship in a row, winning four games to one. Once again, the Warriors were unable to win the title, and Wilt Chamberlain's frustrations continued to grow.

During the 1964-65 basketball season, the Warriors failed to attract large crowds in San Francisco. As a result, the team experienced financial problems. The Warriors could no longer afford to pay Chamberlain's huge salary, which was by far the largest in the league. The team had also drafted Nate Thurmond, a talented young player whose best position was center.

Despite all of Chamberlain's accomplishments, the Warriors decided that their All-Star center was no longer essential to the team. At the 1965 All-Star Game, Wilt was traded to the Philadelphia 76ers. After five and a half seasons with the Warriors, he was headed back to Philadelphia and a new team.

5

I SACRIFICED
MY SCORING

When Wilt Chamberlain joined the Philadelphia 76ers for the last half of the 1964-65 season, he became a member of a solid team with some promising young players. Forwards Luke Jackson and Chet Walker and veteran guards Hal Greer and Larry Costello formed the nucleus of the team. The Sixers, as they were often called, had struggled without a strong center. Chamberlain would fill that role.

After the Warriors had left Philadelphia and moved to San Francisco before the 1962-63 season, the new owners of the Syracuse Nationals moved their team to Philadelphia. They also changed the team's nickname to the 76ers.

Chamberlain was not happy to be traded, and he was even less pleased to be returning to Philadelphia. He briefly considered retiring from basketball, which he could afford to do. He had invested his earnings wisely and was, at 28, wealthy enough that he no longer needed

Philadelphia 76ers coach Alex Hannum talks strategy with Wilt during their championship season.

to play basketball. Sixers co-owner Ike Rich-man, who had been Chamberlain's attorney and friend for several years, persuaded him to join the 76ers and also gave the center a size-able bonus for reporting to the team.

As a 76er, Chamberlain captured his sixth scoring title in his sixth NBA season. Due to injuries and illness, the team struggled after Chamberlain first arrived. Chamberlain had several bouts of pancreatitis, a serious and painful digestive ailment that weakened him and caused him to lose 35 pounds.

The Sixers finished the regular season with only a .500 winning percentage, but their play improved as Chamberlain got used to his new teammates. The team qualified for the playoffs and brushed past the Cincinnati Royals by three games to one. The 76ers next met the Celtics, who were seeking their seventh champion-ship in a row.

Each team won the three games played on its home court, and the seventh game was played in Boston. The Celtics took a seven-point lead with about two minutes left, and they appeared to be headed for the win. But Chamberlain scored six straight points and Boston's lead shrunk to one with five seconds remaining. Bill Russell committed a costly turnover on the inbounds pass, and it was 76er ball with five seconds still to be played. It seemed that the Celtics string of NBA titles might be coming to an end.

In an incredible finish, Celtic forward John Havlicek stole Hal Greer's inbounds pass to Chet Walker and slapped the ball to Boston teammate Sam Jones. Chamberlain could only look on in agony as the game clock ran down.

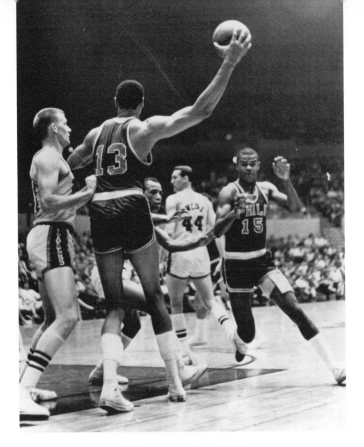

Chamberlain feeds the ball to 76ers teammate Hal Greer (right). A good passer, Wilt led the NBA in assists in 1967–68.

The 76ers had lost to the Celtics one more time.

During the playoff series with Boston, Chamberlain created one of the greatest controversies of his career. He wrote an article for *Sports Illustrated* in which he expressed his views on the NBA and also criticized fellow players, coaches, referees, and sportswriters. He felt that much of the hostility that had been directed at him during his career was caused by jealousy of his accomplishments and his high salary. Treating him as a "villain," Chamberlain said, was easier than appreciating his achievements.

When the article was published in 1965, it was unheard of for athletes to publicly criticize coaches and players, and he angered many people, including his own coach and teammates. It only increased the criticism that Chamberlain received. He was fined by the NBA for his comments.

The 76ers' coach, Dolph Schayes, had been a standout player for 16 seasons. Chamberlain and Schayes did not get along when they played against each other, and Chamberlain had never forgiven Schayes for criticizing him earlier in his career. As player and coach, Chamberlain and Schayes continued to have major differences, and the center had little respect for Schayes's abilities.

In the 1965-66 season, the Sixers played well enough to finish first in the Eastern Division, and Chamberlain had one of his best seasons, winning yet another scoring title and getting chosen the league's most valuable player for the second time. But the Celtics, a proud but aging team, rallied around Coach Red Auerbach, who had announced he would retire after the season. Boston easily defeated Philadelphia in five games. As a result, Schayes was fired, despite having been voted Coach of the Year for his performance in the regular season.

The Sixers new coach for the 1966-67 season was Alex Hannum, who had coached Chamberlain and the Warriors in San Francisco. The Warriors had fired Hannum during his second losing season following Chamberlain's trade to the 76ers. Chamberlain later said when he heard that Hannum was taking over the 76ers he knew the team would win the championship.

The 76ers were the most talented team in the NBA and, with Alex Hannum as coach, they were ready for a great season. Philadelphia had added several gifted young players such as guard Wally Jones and forward Billy Cunningham. In Hal Greer, Chet Walker, and Billy Cunningham, the Sixers had several dependable scorers besides Chamberlain. For the first time in his career, Chamberlain did not have to be his team's leading scorer on a nightly basis. Hannum encouraged him to fill a new role with the Sixers.

Rebounding, passing, and defense became the most important areas of Chamberlain's game, and he was very impressive in his new role as a total team player. For the first time in his career, he did not lead the league in scoring. He averaged only 24 points per game, nine points fewer than the previous year. But because Wilt chose his shots more carefully, he led the league in field goal percentage. And as he made more good passes to teammates, who then made their shots, Chamberlain finished third in the league in assists. This is a remarkable accomplishment for a center.

Chamberlain still had games where he went on a scoring spree, as if to show that he could still do it when he wanted. He later explained, "My scoring went down only because I wanted it to, because it was what was best for my team. I could always score 50-60 points if it was needed, but I knew my team was more effective if I sacrificed my scoring and passed and played defense."

Chamberlain also allowed Hannum to take him out of the game for an occasional rest, a move which he had always disliked in the past. Hannum convinced him that the Sixers were talented enough to afford occasional breaks for Chamberlain. Chamberlain was now 30 years old and suffering from painfully arthritic knees. Hannum believed that his center could play with greater energy and intensity if he took a rest once or twice a game.

Chamberlain did whatever was needed to help his team win. His teammates also performed well in their assigned roles. The result was that the 76ers had one of the best seasons of any team in NBA history. They won 15 of their first 16 games and later put together two winning streaks of 11 games. Their record was 46-4 at the break for the All-Star Game. They dominated every team they played, including the Celtics, and ended the regular season with a 68-13 record, which was then the best in the league's history.

The 76ers continued their excellent play in the playoffs, and they roared through the three rounds with ease. They eliminated the Celtics in five games, ending Boston's run of eight consecutive titles. The Sixers then defeated Chamberlain's old team, the San Francisco Warriors, in the Finals, four games to two. Finally, after so many years of frustration, Wilt Chamberlain had won an NBA championship. His critics could no longer call him a loser.

The 76ers repeated their mastery over the rest of the league in the 1967-68 season, and Chamberlain once again had a fine season in his new team-oriented role. He led the league in assists, which was an amazing feat for a center. But the Sixers stumbled badly in the playoffs, losing to a Celtics team now led by player-coach Bill Russell. It was a disappointing conclusion to another fine season.

The 76ers' reign as one of the NBA's best teams did not last long. Alex Hannum quit the

The 76ers celebrate after finally beating the Celtics, in the 1967 playoffs. Wilt's teammates include (from left) Bob Weiss, Matt Guokas, and Dave Gambee.

club to take a job as general manager and coach of the Oakland Oaks in the new American Basketball Association. Also, after the season, Chamberlain feuded with the team's management over a new contract. Although he had long earned the largest salary in the league, he felt he deserved a hefty raise. The Sixers' management was not willing to meet his demands.

New Philadelphia coach Jack Ramsey did not believe that Chamberlain was well-suited to the style of basketball he wanted the team to play. Feeling unappreciated and growing frustrated with the 76ers management, Chamberlain demanded a trade. The Sixers granted him his wish. Before the 1968-69 season, Chamberlain tried on a new Los Angeles Lakers uniform.

6

A RETURNING HERO

The Lakers had known nothing but disappointment in their quest for an NBA Championship since their move from Minneapolis to Los Angeles in 1960. They had two superstar players in guard Jerry West and forward Elgin Baylor, two of the best players in NBA history. They had won the Western Division title five times in seven years, but had been beaten in the Finals six times by the Celtics and once by the 76ers. The Lakers' biggest problem was that they had never had a dominating center. With the trade for Wilt Chamberlain before the 1968-69 season, their need was finally met.

A number of talented centers had come into the NBA in the years that Chamberlain had dominated the league, players who possessed the height, athletic ability, strength, and basketball skills. Walt Bellamy, Nate Thurmond, Willis Reed, Elvin Hayes, and Wes Unseld had

Chamberlain played a different type of basketball as a Laker. But he could always score—here, over Elvin Hayes of the Houston Rockets.

Touching his injured knee, Chamberlain vows to come back from knee surgery in time for the 1970 playoffs— and he did.

all followed Chamberlain's example to become dominating centers. But even at age 32, Chamberlain was still the best in the league. While his arthritic knees somewhat limited his speed and mobility, he had spent years working out with weights to add much upper body strength to his already impressive physique. His added strength helped him in his oncourt battles with these strong young centers.

Chamberlain was happy to be back in California. He had enjoyed his stint with the Warriors in San Francisco. He had come to like the Los Angeles area as well. The warm California weather and active lifestyle particularly appealed to him. His parents also moved there, in the months before his father passed away in October 1968.

Fitting Chamberlain's talent and personality into an established team like the Lakers was difficult. West and Baylor were effective offensive players who had their own styles and habits. With Chamberlain's arrival, these two veterans were forced to make major changes in their own play.

The Lakers' coach was Butch Van Breda Kolff, who had been an accomplished coach at Princeton University for many years before coming to Los Angeles. He was a strong personality, an outspoken coach who made certain that his players knew that he was the boss. He was exactly the type of coach that Chamberlain had never gotten along with. The two men disliked each other immediately, and they fought throughout the season. Chamberlain thought little of Van Breda Kolff's abilities, calling the him "the worst coach I ever had."

Despite these problems, the Lakers captured the Western Division title in the regular season. Chamberlain scored a career low of 20.5 points per game, but led the league in rebounds and field goal percentage.

In the playoffs, the Lakers met the Celtics in the finals. Los Angeles took a 3-2 lead in the series, then lost the last two games, including the final game at home. In the last game, with about five minutes to play, Chamberlain had to leave the game with a slight injury. He was quickly able to return and told his coach he was ready to go back in, but Van Breda Kolff kept him on the bench and ignored his requests to return to play. The coach kept his star center out of the game, as the clock ran down and the contest slipped away. Boston beat Los Angeles by two points. Chamberlain was infuriated by Van Breda Kolff's decisions.

Besides the disappointment of another loss

in the final round of the playoffs, the contest also marked the last game of Bill Russell as both player and coach. The great Chamberlain-Russell battles were over, with a frustrated Chamberlain having lost to Russell's Celtics in seven of their eight playoff meetings.

Van Breda Kolff quit the Lakers coaching job before the 1969-70 season and was replaced by former Providence College coach Joe Mullaney, who had a much calmer relationship with Chamberlain. In their first season together, however, they faced a major ordeal. In November, only nine games into the season, Chamberlain was running upcourt when his right knee suddenly gave way, and he fell to the floor in agony. He had torn a tendon in the knee, his first serious injury ever.

Chamberlain underwent surgery to repair the damage the next day. Normally, it took a long period of rehabilitation to recover from the operation. Some doctors feared he might never recover fully. Even the most optimistic ones predicted that he would be out for at least the rest of the season. But Chamberlain had other plans. He saw the rehabilitation process as a personal challenge and decided that he would return in time for the playoffs, which began in late March. Almost every expert thought that this was impossible.

After eight weeks, the cast came off his leg, and Chamberlain began a tedious and painful program of whirlpool exercises, weight lifting, bicycling, and running. Whatever goals were set for him in his rehab activities, Chamberlain doubled the amount. For example, if he was asked to do 10 lifts, he would do 20. If he was told to run one mile, he would run at least two. (He enjoyed running on the beach, where he also discovered the pleasures of playing volleyball.)

By March, Chamberlain had recovered sufficiently to begin workouts with the Lakers, and he met his goal of returning for the playoffs. Chamberlain's rapid recovery was an incredible achievement, a tribute to his will and determination. The significance of his accomplishment was not lost on basketball fans, who treated the center like a returning hero.

His courageous and successful effort to return made Chamberlain seem more human and likable, and fans began to treat him more warmly than he had ever been treated before. He finally achieved the popular acceptance he had sought for so long but had never received.

Although Chamberlain was not completely healthy yet, he and the Lakers were playing well as the regular

Nate Thurmond sets a pick on the Lakers' Pat Riley (yes, that Pat Riley), but Jeff Mullins is about to have his shot blocked by Wilt Chamberlain, playing in his final postseason.

season ended and the playoffs began. Los Angeles met the New York Knicks in the finals. In a thrilling series that lasted seven games, the Knicks overcame an injury to center Willis Reed and defeated the Lakers. Chamberlain did not play at his usual level, and some people, forgetting that he was still recovering from his own injury, blamed him for the loss. It was a disappointing end to the season, but Chamberlain and the Lakers seemed to be on their way to becoming the overpowering team many had expected them to become.

The 1970-71 season was a major disappointment for the Lakers. West and Baylor were injured much of the year, and Coach Joe Mullaney was forced to use young, less-experienced players. Chamberlain played well, concentrating again on defense and rebounding while scoring a career low of "just" 20.7 points per game. The Lakers were eliminated from the playoffs by the Milwaukee Bucks, who were led by center Lew Alcindor. Alcindor, who would later change his name to Kareem Abdul-Jabbar, was the best center to join the NBA since Chamberlain.

In 1971, Chamberlain built an incredible house on a hilltop in the posh community of Bel Air. The house, which cost several million dollars, was built to his specifications and was shaped like a modern pyramid. It included enormous windows that offered spectacular views in every direction of the Los Angeles area, and an indoor-outdoor swimming pool that surrounded the house on several sides.

Bill Sharman took over the Lakers for the 1971-72 season. Sharman, once a star player with the Celtics, had a record of success as an NBA coach. He took the trouble to build a healthy relationship with Chamberlain. As a result, Chamberlain cooperated with Sharman, even attending practice sessions on game days, which he had previously refused to do.

The season started, and the Lakers finally began to meet the high expectations that many had for them. Sharman encouraged an up-tempo style of play that would utilize Chamberlain's rebounding and passing skills. Jerry West handled the playmaking responsibilities, while the other guard, Gail Goodrich, was the team's top scorer. Elgin Baylor retired early in the year, his knees too damaged to allow him to continue to play, but the Lakers had solid players who were capable of replacing Baylor's scoring. Sharman's new approach proved effective, and the Lakers soon emerged as the best team in the NBA.

The Lakers tore through the league, winning an all-time record of 33 consecutive games at one point. They ended the season at 69-13, the best regular-season mark in NBA history, breaking the record that Chamberlain's 76ers had set in the 1966-67 season. Chamberlain, now the Lakers' team captain, had another great season. His scoring dropped to 14.8 points per game, but he contributed in many other ways. Sharman later remarked, "He just did everything I wanted him to do and he did a tremendous job."

The Lakers' success continued in the playoffs, as they eliminated the Chicago Bulls and Milwaukee Bucks. In the Finals, Chamberlain and his team destroyed the New York Knicks in five games. Chamberlain played brilliantly, despite breaking his hand in the fourth game of the Finals. Despite the terrible pain from his injury, he scored 24 points, grabbed 29 rebounds, and blocked 10 shots in the fifth and final game. He was simply unstoppable. The Lakers triumphed, 114-100.

The Los Angeles Lakers had finally won their first championship. For his outstanding performance, Chamberlain was named the NBA Finals' Most Valuable Player.

Chamberlain led the Lakers into the NBA finals again the following season, and this time they lost to New York in five games. No one except Chamberlain knew it at the time, but it was the last game for the NBA's greatest center.

7

AFTER THE GAME

Wilt Chamberlain retired after 14 seasons in the NBA with a scoring average of 30.1 points per game. He had grabbed 23,924 rebounds. He had led the league in scoring in seven consecutive seasons and in rebounding in 11 seasons. Chamberlain had won four Most Valuable Player awards and had been selected to play in 13 All-Star Games. Remarkably, he had never fouled out of an NBA game, despite his often physical style of play and having played an average of nearly 46 minutes per game during his career. Most importantly, he had led teams to two NBA Championships. Chamberlain was elected to the Basketball Hall of Fame in 1978.

The year following his retirement from the Lakers, Chamberlain accepted an offer to become the player-coach of the San Diego Conquistadors of the American Basketball Associa-

Owner Leonard Bloom is all smiles as Wilt announces that he has signed on to be player-coach of the San Diego Conquistadors.

tion. The Lakers, however, held his rights to play for one more season, and they prevented him from playing for the San Diego team. He sued the Lakers, and the matter ended up in court for several years.

Chamberlain coached the Conquistadors for one season, and he was not very good at the job. He hated attending team practices as much while coaching as he had as a player, and he often had his assistant coach supervise the sessions while Chamberlain was someplace else. Because of personal business, he even missed several games, which is unheard of behavior for a coach. The Conquistadors had a poor record, and Chamberlain lost interest in coaching as the year reached its conclusion, when he quit.

Chamberlain was in good shape when he left basketball, and he remained physically active even in retirement. Every few years, until he was nearly 50 years old, NBA teams would contact him about emerging from retirement and returning to basketball. No one expected him to be the dominating player of his youth, but he probably could have played adequately in a limited role. Chamberlain was intrigued by these offers and gave consideration to several of them, but he turned all of them down. He did not seem to miss the sport he had dominated for so long.

Chamberlain pursued a variety of activities in retirement. He organized and played in a professional volleyball league, in which he was an outstanding player. He also became an enthusiastic tennis player and was often seen in the crowd at major tennis tournaments. Chamberlain continued his frequent and widespread travels around the world. Still enjoying the single life, he has never married.

One of the first athletes to earn the large salaries that later became common in professional sports, Wilt Chamberlain invested his earnings intelligently and retired from basketball a wealthy man. He is a good businessman and spends much of his time overseeing his many successful interests.

Even more than 20 years after his retirement from basketball, Wilt Chamberlain's accomplishments remain impressive. More than any other player, Chamberlain changed the sport of basketball. Before his arrival, basketball was a slow and methodical sport that could often be very dull. With his immense talent, Chamberlain demonstrated that a single gifted player can determine the style and pace of the game.

In the first half of his career, Chamberlain was the greatest scorer and rebounder who had ever played in the NBA. He was the first player to regularly use the slam dunk as an offensive weapon, arguably the most exciting shot in basketball. Later in his career, Chamberlain changed his style of play and demonstrated that he could be just as effective as an unselfish defensive specialist, sacrificing his own shot opportunities for the good of his team.

Chamberlain, outside his Bel Air, California, estate with Great Danes Careem, Thor, and Odin.

The outstanding centers who followed Chamberlain in the NBA were expected to follow his example and be superior athletes who were effective on both offense and defense. Kareem Abdul-Jabbar, Hakeem Olajuwon, Patrick Ewing, David Robinson, and Shaquille O'Neal are the best of the centers who came after Chamberlain, yet none of these talented players have surpassed Chamberlain's achievements on the court.

Some of the records that Chamberlain held when he retired have been surpassed by other players. Abdul-Jabbar bettered Chamberlain's career marks for total points and rebounds largely because he played six more seasons than Chamberlain.

Guard Michael Jordan, who dominated the NBA during his career much as Chamberlain did during his, is the only player to surpass Chamberlain's career scoring average. Jordan also tied Chamberlain's record of seven consecutive NBA scoring titles. No one has come close to breaking three of Chamberlain's records, all of which were set during his magnificent 1961-62 season: highest scoring average in a season (50.4), most points in a season (4,029), and most points in a single game (100). Chamberlain also still holds the record for most rebounds in a game with the astounding total of 55.

Few athletes have dominated their sport as completely as Chamberlain ruled the world of basketball. He will always be considered one of the best ever to play the game.

STATISTICS

WILTON NORMAN CHAMBERLAIN

SEASON	TEAM	G	MIN	FGA	FGM	PCT	FTA	FTM	PCT	RBD	AST	PTS	AVG
59-60	Phila	72	**3338**	2311	1065	.461	991	577	.582	**1941**	168	**2707**	**37.6**
60-61	Phila	79	**3773**	2457	1251	**.509**	1054	531	.504	**2149**	148	**3033**	**38.4**
61-62	Phila	80	**3882**	3159	1597	.506	1363	835	.613	**2052**	192	**4029**	**50.4**
62-63	SF	80	**3806**	2770	1463	**.528**	1113	660	.593	**1946**	275	**3586**	**44.8**
63-64	SF	80	**3689**	2298	1204	.524	1016	540	.531	1787	403	**2948**	**36.9**
64-65	SF/Ph	73	3301	2083	1063	**.510**	880	408	.464	1673	250	**2534**	**34.7**
65-66	Phila	79	**3737**	1990	1074	**.540**	976	501	.513	**1943**	414	**2649**	**33.5**
66-67	Phila	81	**3682**	1150	785	**.683**	875	386	.441	**1957**	630	1956	24.1
67-68	Phila	82	**3836**	1377	819	**.595**	932	354	.380	**1952**	**702**	1992	24.3
68-69	LA	81	3669	1099	641	**.583**	857	382	.446	**1712**	366	1664	20.5
69-70	LA	12	505	227	129	.568	157	70	.446	221	49	328	27.3
70-71	LA	82	3630	1226	668	.545	669	360	.538	**1493**	352	1696	20.7
71-72	LA	82	3469	764	496	**.649**	524	221	.422	**1572**	329	1213	14.8
72-73	LA	82	3542	586	426	**.727**	455	232	.510	**1526**	365	1084	13.2

Regular													
Season Totals		1045	47859	23497	12681	.540	11862	6057	.511	23924	4643	31419	30.1
Playoff Totals		160	7559	2728	1425	.522	1627	757	.465	3913	673	3607	22.5
All-Star Totals		13	388	122	72	.590	94	47	.500	197	36	191	14.7

G   games
MIN   minutes
FGA   field goals attempted
FGM   field goals made
PCT   percent
FTA   free throws attempted
FTM   free throws made
RBD   rebounds
AST   assists
PTS   points
AVG   scoring average

Records still held:

most points, one game: 100
most rebounds, one game: 55
highest scoring average, one season: 50.4
most points, one season: 4029
most rebounds, one season: 2149
most games, never fouled out, career: 1045

bold indicates league-leading figures

WILT CHAMBERLAIN:
A CHRONOLOGY

1936   Born August 21 in Philadelphia

1951   YMCA team wins national championship

1955   Graduates from Overbrook High School and enters Kansas University

1957   Leads Kansas Jayhawks to NCAA championship game, where they lose to the University of North Carolina Tarheels

1958   Leaves Kansas and joins the Harlem Globetrotters

1959-60   Joins the Philadelphia Warriors, where he wins Most Valuable Player and Rookie of the Year Awards

1961-62   Averages 50.4 points per game; sets record by scoring 100 points in a single game

1962-63   Moves to San Francisco with the Warriors

1964-65   Traded to the Philadelphia 76ers at midseason

1966-67   Leads the 76ers to a 68-13 record and the NBA Championship; wins fourth Most Valuable Player Award

1968-69   Traded to the Los Angeles Lakers

1969-70   Suffers serious knee injury; returns less than four months later for playoffs

1971-72   Leads the Lakers to a 69-13 record—the best in NBA history—and the NBA Championship

1972-73   Retires after 14th NBA season

1973-74   Coaches the San Diego Conquistadors of the American Basketball Association

1978   Elected to the Basketball Hall of Fame

SUGGESTIONS FOR FURTHER READING

Chamberlain, Wilt, with David Shaw. *Wilt.* Macmillan: New York, 1973.

Chamberlain, Wilt. *A View from Above.* Penguin: New York, 1991.

George, Nelson. *Elevating the Game.* Simon & Schuster: New York, 1992.

Hollander, Zander, and Sachare, Alex, eds. *The Official NBA Basketball Encyclopedia.* Villard: New York, 1989.

Libby, Bill. *Goliath: The Wilt Chamberlain Story.* Dodd, Mead & Co.: New York, 1977.

Nadel, Eric. *The Night Wilt Scored 100.* Taylor Publishing: Dallas, Texas, 1990.

Pluto, Terry. *Tall Tales.* Simon & Schuster: New York, 1992.

Shapiro, Miles. *Bill Russell: Basketball Great.* Chelsea House: New York, 1991.

INDEX

Abdul-Jabbar, Kareem, 54–60
Allen, Phog, 22, 26–7
Attles, Al, 13, 37
Auerbach, Red, 23, 34, 44
Baylor, Elgin, 49, 50, 54–5
Bellamy, Walt, 49
Boston Celtics, 12, 34, 37, 39, 42–3, 44, 46, 49, 51, 54
Big Eight Conference, 27
Bloom, Leonard, 56
Brennan, Pete, 29
Chamberlain, Olivia, 17, 50
Chamberlain, William, 17, 50
Chamberlain, Wilt
  as a coach, 58
  as a free-throw shooter, 34, 36
  as a rookie, 33–4, 35
  as a tennis player, 58
  as a track star, 16, 19
  as a volleyball player, 58
  All-NBA team, 33, 57
  elected to Hall of Fame, 57
  faces discrimination, 25–6
  illness and injuries, 42, 46, 50, 51, 52–3
  Most Valuable Player Award, 33, 57
  NBA Finals' Most Valuable Player, 55
  record-setting performances, 9–15, 60
  retirement, 57, 58
  rookie of the year, 33
  signing autographs, 37
  social life of, 38, 50, 59
Chicago Bulls, 55
Cincinnati Royals, 42
Costello, Larry, 41
Cousy, Bob, 34
Cunningham, Billy, 45

Ewing, Patrick, 60
FBI, 22
Feerick, Bob, 38
Gambee, Dave, 47
Goodrich, Gail, 54
Gottlieb, Eddie, 23, 30, 38
Greer, Hal, 41, 42, 43, 45
Guokas, Matt, 47
Hannum, Alex, 38–9, 40, 44, 46
Harlem Globetrotters, 31, 38
Harp, Dick, 27, 30
Havlicek, John, 42
Hayes, Elvin, 48, 49
Imhoff, Darrell, 11
Jackson, Luke, 41
Johnston, Neil, 13, 34, 36, 37
Jones, Sam, 42
Jones, Wally, 45
Jordan, Michael, 60
Kansas Jayhawks, 27–30, 36
Kansas University, 22, 25–6
Kutsher's Country Club, 23
Lawrence, Kansas, 25, 26
Loneski, Ron, 29
Los Angeles Lakers, 47, 49–52, 53, 55, 57–8
Maravich, Pete, 15
McGuire, Frank, 13, 28–9, 36, 38
Meschery, Tom, 37
Michigan State University, 28
Mikan, George, 12
Milwaukee Bucks, 54, 55
Mullany, Joe, 52, 54
Mullins, Jeff, 53
Naismith, Dr. James, 22
NBA rules, 23, 30, 35
NCAA, 22
NCAA tournament, 28
New York Knicks, 9, 11, 53, 55
North Carolina Tarheels, 28–30, 36

Oakland Oaks, 47
Olajuwon, Hakeem, 60
O'Neal, Shaquille, 60
Overbrook High School, 20, 21, 22
Philadelphia, Pennsylvania, 17, 20, 25
Philadelphia 76ers, 39, 41–47, 49, 55
Philadelphia Warriors, 23, 30, 31, 33, 34, 35, 37
Princeton University, 51
Providence University, 52
Quigg, Joe, 30
Ramsey, Jack, 47
Reed, Willis, 49, 53
Richman, Ike, 42
Riley, Pat, 53
Robinson, David, 60
Rodgers, Guy, 13, 37
Rosenbluth, Lenny, 29
Rucklick, Joe, 14
Russell, Bill, 12, 32, 34–5, 39, 42, 46, 52
San Diego Conquistadors, 57–8
San Francisco Warriors, 38–9, 44, 46, 50
Saperstein, Abe, 30–1,
Schayes, Dolph, 44
Sharman, Bill, 54–5
slam dunk, 59
Sports Illustrated, 43
Syracuse Nationals, 36
Thompson, David, 15
Thurmond, Nate, 39, 49, 53
University of San Francisco, 28
Unseld, Wes, 49
Van Breda Kolff, Butch, 51, 52
Walker, Chet, 41, 42, 45
Weiss, Bob, 47
West, Jerry, 49, 50, 54
YMCA championship, 20

ABOUT THE AUTHOR

Ron Frankl is a graduate of Haverford College. He is the author of *Duke Ellington* and *Charlie Parker* for Chelsea House Publishers' "Black Americans of Achievement" series and *Bruce Springsteen* for the "Popular Culture" series. During basketball season, Mr. Frankl's happiness is largely determined by the successes and failures of the New York Knicks.